Remembering the Past

Remembering the Past

Reproduction Quilts Inspired by Antique Favorites

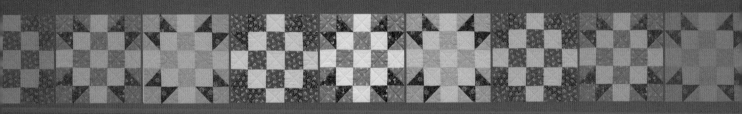

JULIE HENDRICKSEN

Martingale®
Create with Confidence

Dedication

*To my son, Matt. You are just the person I had hoped you
would grow into—kind, thoughtful, and the best dad for Alex.
I am very proud of you.*

Remembering the Past: Reproduction Quilts
Inspired by Antique Favorites
© 2015 by Julie Hendricksen

Martingale®
19021 120th Ave. NE, Ste. 102
Bothell, WA 98011-9511 USA
ShopMartingale.com

Printed in China
20 19 18 17 16 15   8 7 6 5 4 3 2 1

**Library of Congress Cataloging-in-Publication Data
is available upon request.**

ISBN: 978-1-60468-709-5

Mission Statement

Dedicated to providing quality products
and service to inspire creativity.

Credits

PUBLISHER AND CHIEF VISIONARY OFFICER
Jennifer Erbe Keltner

EDITORIAL DIRECTOR
Karen Costello Soltys

DESIGN DIRECTOR
Paula Schlosser

ACQUISITIONS EDITOR
Karen M. Burns

PHOTOGRAPHER
Brent Kane

TECHNICAL EDITOR
Monique Dillard

PRODUCTION MANAGER
Regina Girard

COPY EDITOR
Marcy Heffernan

ILLUSTRATOR
Anne Moscicki

～ Contents ～

ꗬ Introduction ꗭ

I have a confession to make. I've been collecting antique quilts for more than 30 years and at last count, I owned more than 200 of them. Yet I can't resist seeking out antique quilts and textiles. Why?

Because each one is so fascinating. And the closer you look, the more interesting they become. Over the years I've discovered so many unique prints (have you ever seen a French horn print?), unusual fabric pairings, faded colors that intrigue me, and distinctive settings or borders. All of this has helped me build a wealth of knowledge. I'm not an expert—I'm not a certified appraiser or anything like that. I just collect what I like and, honestly, my taste in quilts hasn't changed much over the years.

While I own quilts from other eras, scrap quilts stitched at the end of the nineteenth century (1870s to the 1890s) are my favorites. I love to display them and decorate with them and investigate the fabrics up close. Many of my collected antique quilts have become the inspiration behind the fabrics I've designed for Windham Fabrics. I also own a quilt shop, JJ Stitches, in Sun Prairie, Wisconsin, that specializes in reproduction fabrics because so many quilters— like you and like me—also love the quilts of this era.

Whether it's the colors (think blue, indigo, red, double pink, black, gray, brown, and shirting prints), the traditional patchwork designs, or the unique or "renegade" nature of some of the quilt blocks, these old quilts speak to me. And I'm pretty sure they speak to you, too.

With a large collection of antique quilts, you may be wondering why I make reproduction ones. The patterns in this book showcase how I

reinterpret an antique quilt when making my "modern" version. I scrutinize the colors and patterns of the fabrics and how they're combined. And I consider what really is special about each of those quilts. In the end, I may use fewer colors, make the new quilt a slightly different size, or even reverse the darks and lights to create a completely different-looking quilt. (For more about the fabrics, turn to "In Love with Reproduction Fabrics" on page 9.)

Some of my color choices (or more specifically, the limits I put on my color choices) are to make it easier for quilters to reproduce a pattern. Rather than using 100 or more bits and pieces, I may select 30 or 40 prints. That means you can start with fat eighths or fat quarters to make the quilt top. Quite frequently, I also simplify the background, using one or two light shirting prints rather than dozens. Of course, if you have a huge stash and want to incorporate 100 prints in your quilts, go right ahead!

Another special feature of this book is that both versions of the quilts—the antique and the made-to-look-like-old quilts—are photographed together. That way you can easily see just how alike or different they are. Close-up photos of some of the old blocks let you really see what the fabrics were like. (And yes, one of the quilts really does have a French horn print in it. See if you can find it! Hint: it's on page 18.)

I invite you to brew a cup of coffee or mug of tea, get situated in your most comfortable chair, and spend some time perusing the pages of this book. Enjoy discovering which patterns are your favorites, and then imagine the fun you'll have selecting reproduction prints and lovingly stitching them together into a quilt that will surely become an heirloom for your family.

~ Julie

Reproduction fabrics, more specifically those that represent the late nineteenth century, have been quite popular for years. So popular, in fact, that just about every fabric company offers at least one designer collection of them each year. If you're new to reproductions or just want to learn a bit more about chrome yellow, double pinks, Lancaster blue, or the various types of prints popular at the time, this section is for you.

Every Era Has Its Colors

When you think about it, every era, including the one we're in now, has its popular or signature colors. Gray—from the palest dove gray to the deepest charcoal—is quite in vogue today. Well, it was the same in the late 1800s. Certain colors were prevalent; others were nonexistent. One predominant reason for this was that manufacturers had to use the dyes that were available to them. Unlike today, many of the dyes were plant or natural element based rather than chemical based. Often the dyes weren't stable and colors tended to fade or change over time. The dyes that held true, like indigos and chrome yellows, became a big part of the color story of the late nineteenth century. Let's take a closer look at what was "hot" back then.

Indigos

Indigo is dark, vivid blue, originally created from plant material native to the tropics and Asia. Today, almost all indigo fabrics (think blue jeans!) are dyed using synthetic dyes. Back in the day, the dyeing process was all natural.

Whether used to create small shirting prints on cream backgrounds or to make deep, rich blue fabrics, this color is one of the most prominent seen in quilts in the 1800s—pre– and post–Civil War.

Madder and Turkey Reds

Madder is another plant-based dye, one that turns fibers a deep red or russet color. Madder wasn't the most stable of dyes, so often fabrics dyed with this plant faded or turned colors over time. Some antique fabrics that look tan or faded olive green probably started out life as a rusty red.

Turkey red also has its foundation in madder, but through a unique and laborious process, the red dyes that originated in the Middle East remained vivid over time. Turkey red doesn't relate to a specific shade of red; it's the generic term Europeans gave to red fabrics printed by this Middle Eastern process.

Madder reds

Indigos

Turkey reds

Double Pinks

Sometimes called "bubblegum pink," the true pink prints of this era were double pinks. (Bubblegum pink was more prevalent during the 1920s and '30s.) Double pinks were created by printing dark pink or red over a lighter shade of pink onto the base fabric, giving the fabric more depth while also maintaining the overall pink color. From little ditzy prints to wallpaper-type stripes, these fabrics seem to lift a quilt from somber to something a bit more fun.

Lancaster and Cadet Blues

Like double pinks, medium-blue fabrics that were printed double (darker blue over a lighter shade) were popular in the 1800s. Why they weren't commonly called "double blues" is unknown, but perhaps the name Lancaster blue stuck because this color was so popular among Pennsylvania quiltmakers at that time. Like double pinks, Lancaster blue fabrics most often featured small-scale close-together motifs.

Cadet blue, by comparison, is deeper than the light Lancaster blue, but not as dark as indigo. Often cadet blue prints had small white motifs enhancing the designs.

Chrome Yellows and Poison Greens

Two common fabric colors of the nineteenth century are vivid chrome yellow (named for the naturally occurring chromium) and poison green (a bright yellow-green sometimes called acid green that originated by using copper arsenate—arsenic!). You won't find much of either of these colors in the quilts in this book. It's just not that common to find antique quilts featuring these colors, but you may find them perfectly lovely and want to incorporate them into some of your reproduction quilts.

Mourning Grays

Given that this time was one of great sorrow and mourning in the United States following the Civil War, mourning grays were a popular color choice for clothing—which often meant that the scraps went into quilts. After a one-year period of wearing black with no adornment while mourning the loss of a spouse or loved one, the fashion of the day dictated that women would spend the subsequent six months in a period of half mourning. Gray prints, which were often black on gray or gray on purple, were called half-mourning prints or mourning grays. Somber in color, these fabrics did allow for subtle prints.

Fugitive Purples

Believe it or not, purples were a popular color choice during the nineteenth century. We just don't see much evidence of them because they were made with highly unstable dyes, referred to as "fugitive." The purples frequently faded to browns and tans, and were highly susceptible to change when exposed to sunlight. Purples were often used with mourning grays and blacks.

Double pinks   Cheddar and chrome yellow   Mourning grays

Cadet blues   Poison greens   Fugitive purples

It's All about the Prints

Well, maybe it's not *all* about the prints, but let's face it, one of the things we love about antique quilts is the diversity of the prints and what fabric manufacturers decided to print on their wares. While color tells the immediate story when you look at a quilt, part of the fun is in the close inspection to see the actual motifs printed on the fabrics.

Shirtings

Look at any quilt from the late nineteenth century and you're likely to find something interesting about the "background" fabrics. They're printed, typically on an off-white or cream base (or maybe that's just the shade that the original white fabric turned with time) with tiny prints that replicate the look of men's shirting fabrics. Or do they remind you more of pajamas?

Shirting prints often were printed in a striped pattern, where the stripes weren't made simply of solid lines. Today, we often use the term shirtings to mean any small motif printed in black or indigo or even red on a cream background. But many of these prints that are scattered in an allover pattern were called "ditzy" prints. See below for more on them.

Ditzy Prints

From dots to arrows to tiny leaves or flowers, ditzy prints are allover motifs. They may be dark colors printed on cream, like shirtings. Or, they may reveal white showing through a darker color like indigo or cadet blue.

Printed Stripes

As bold as wallpaper, printed stripes in the 1800s were multicolored, mixed wide stripes with narrow ones, and often featured a combination of big motifs with smaller ones. If one could afford this type of fabric, it was most often used for sashing and borders.

Paisleys and Florals

Just as common today as 150 years ago, both paisleys and floral prints were popular during the Civil War era. Large or small, they are timeless motifs.

Plaids, Checks, and Geometrics

When you take a close look at some of the antique quilts in this book, you'll notice that quite a few of them incorporated plaids and checks or other geometric prints. Remember, quiltmakers at that time did not have the advantages we enjoy today, like rotary cutters, accurate rulers, and endless fabric choices at our favorite local quilt shop. When they used bits of plaid, the bits were often off-kilter. Some of us today would cringe at the thought. Back then? They used what they had and were most likely glad of it!

Shirtings

Printed stripes

Ditzy prints

Paisleys and florals

Plaids, checks, and geometrics

Given the plethora of antique star quilts, star blocks were likely as popular in the 1800s as they are today. I love the elements of surprise this quilt holds when it is folded on the shelf. It's not until you unfurl it that you see the vibrant inner border and striped binding (which is the backing fabric turned to the front).

A red inner border adds a pop of color to the antique quilt.

Did the original quiltmaker intentionally alter the direction of her plaids for added interest?

She must have had plenty of the plaid used in the center square, since it appears often in the quilt top.

Switching to high-contrast lights and darks surrounding the star changes the block's look entirely.

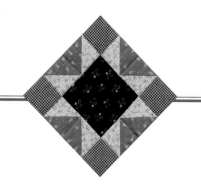

Present-day quilters sometimes feel they have to make a color choice, deciding between black and blue. This quilt proves that black and blue can pair nicely together—eliminating the need to choose at all!

"Stars on the Prairie"
Finished quilt: 67" x 78⅜"
Finished block: 8" x 8"

Materials

Yardage is based on 42"-wide fabric. Fat eighths are 9" x 21".

3⅓ yards of pink print for setting squares, setting triangles, and outer border

12 fat eighths of assorted indigo prints for blocks

8 fat eighths of assorted plaids for blocks

3 fat eighths of assorted black prints for blocks

10 fat eighths of assorted light shirting prints for blocks

½ yard of white shirting print for inner border

⅔ yard of navy print for binding

5 yards of fabric for backing

79" x 91" piece of cotton batting

Cutting

From the pink print, cut:

5 strips, 8½" x 42"; crosscut into 20 squares, 8½" x 8½"

2 strips, 12¾" x 42"; crosscut into 5 squares, 12¾" x 12¾". Cut squares into quarters diagonally to yield 20 triangles. (You'll have 2 left over.)

1 strip, 9½" x 42"; crosscut into 2 squares, 9½" x 9½". Cut squares in half diagonally to yield 4 triangles.

8 strips, 4" x 42"

From 8 of the indigo prints, cut:

3 strips, 2½" x 21"; crosscut into:
    8 rectangles, 2½" x 4½" (64 total)
    8 squares, 2½" x 2½" (64 total)

From 3 of the indigo prints, cut:

3 strips, 2½" x 21"; crosscut into 12 rectangles, 2½" x 4½" (36 total)

From 1 of the indigo prints, cut:

1 strip, 2½" x 21"; crosscut into 8 squares, 2½" x 2½"

From 6 of the plaids, cut:

1 strip, 4½" x 21"; crosscut into 4 squares, 4½" x 4½" (24 total)

1 strip, 2½" x 21"; crosscut into 4 squares, 2½" x 2½" (24 total)

From 2 of the plaids, cut:

1 strip, 4½" x 21"; crosscut into:
    2 squares, 4½" x 4½" (4 total)
    4 rectangles 2½" x 4½" (8 total)

1 strip, 2½" x 21"; crosscut into 8 squares, 2½" x 2½" (16 total)

From *1* of the black prints, cut:
1 strip, 4½" x 21"; crosscut into:
    2 squares, 4½" x 4½"
    4 rectangles, 2½" x 4½"

From *2* of the black prints, cut:
2 strips, 2½" x 21"; crosscut into:
    4 rectangles, 2½" x 4½" (8 total)
    4 squares, 2½" x 2½" (8 total)

From *each* of the light shirting prints, cut:
3 strips, 2½" x 21"; crosscut into 24 squares,
    2½" x 2½" (240 total)

From the white shirting print, cut:
6 strips, 2" x 42"

From the navy print for binding, cut:
7 strips, 2½" x 42"

> ## Keeping Count
> From the indigo prints, plaids, and black
> prints (collectively referred to as "darks" in
> the instructions), you should have a total of:
> * 120 rectangles, 2½" x 4½"
> * 120 squares, 2½" x 2½"
> * 30 squares, 4½" x 4½"

Making the Blocks

Instructions are for making one block at a time so
that you can easily keep the pieces organized. For each
block you'll need four matching dark rectangles, four
matching 2½" squares from a different dark fabric, and
one dark 4½" square from a third dark fabric. You'll
also need eight matching light shirting 2½" squares.

1. Draw a diagonal line from corner to corner on the
   wrong side of the light shirting 2½" squares.

2. Place a marked light square on one end of a dark
   2½" x 4½" rectangle as shown with right sides
   together. Stitch directly on the line; trim away the
   excess fabric, leaving a ¼" seam allowance. Press the
   seam allowances toward the light print.

3. In the same manner, place a second marked light
   2½" square at the opposite end of the 2½" x 4½"
   rectangle as shown. Sew directly on the line, trim
   as before, and press the seam allowances toward the
   light print. Repeat to make four flying-geese units.

Make 4.

4. Lay out four flying-geese units, four dark 2½"
   squares, and one plaid or black 4½" square in
   three horizontal rows. Join the units and squares
   into rows; press the seam allowances toward the
   dark squares. Join the rows to make a Sawtooth
   Star block. Press the seam allowances as shown.
   The block should measure 8½" x 8½". Repeat to
   make a total of 30 Sawtooth Star blocks, varying
   the dark prints.

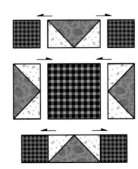 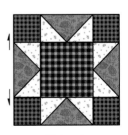

Make 30.

Assembling the Quilt Top

1. Lay out the Sawtooth Star blocks, pink 8½" squares, pink side setting triangles, and pink corner triangles in 12 diagonal rows.

2. Sew the pieces together into rows. Press the seam allowances toward the pink print.

3. Join the rows to complete the quilt center. Press the seam allowances in one direction.

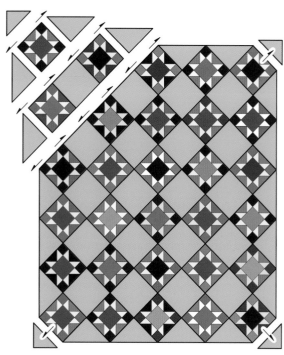

Quilt assembly

Adding the Borders

1. Sew two white-shirting 2" x 42" strips together end to end using a diagonal seam to make a long border strip. Repeat with two more strips. Measure the length of the quilt top through the center, and cut the two strips to this length. Sew them to the sides of the quilt top, pressing the seam allowances toward the border.

2. Using the two remaining white-shirting 2" x 42" strips, measure the width of the quilt top through the center, and cut the strips to this length. Sew them to the top and bottom of the quilt top, pressing the seam allowances toward the border.

3. Sew two pink 4" x 42" strips together end to end using a diagonal seam to make a long border strip. Repeat with two more strips. Measure the length

of the quilt top through the center, and cut the two strips to this length. Sew them to the sides of the quilt top, pressing the seam allowances toward the pink border.

4. Join two of the remaining pink 4" x 42" strips with a diagonal seam. Repeat with the remaining pink strips. Measure the width of the quilt top through the center, and cut the strips to this length. Sew them to the top and bottom of the quilt top. Press the seam allowances toward the pink border.

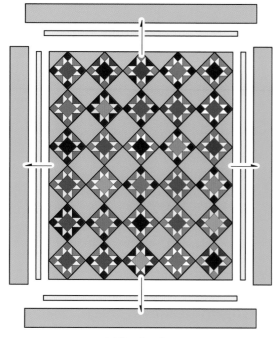

Adding borders

Finishing the Quilt

For more information on finishing your quilt, see ShopMartingale.com/HowtoQuilt.

1. Layer the backing, batting, and quilt top; baste.

2. Quilt as you wish. The quilt shown was quilted in a 2"-wide diagonal grid.

3. Bind the quilt using the navy-print 2½"-wide strips.

Re-creating the Past

I wash my quilts after quilting to further shrink the fabric and batting. This gives them an antique look.

Darting Bird blocks are flying in formation in diagonal bands of classic late-19th-century colors—indigo, burgundy, gray, brown, red, black, and double pink. The faded rows were likely stronger in contrast when the quilt was made, but time, unstable dyes, and perhaps sunlight have since caused the fabrics to lose their pigment. If you're curious about my name for the quilt, turn the Darting Bird blocks 180°; don't they resemble little men-at-work icons?

Borderless quilts weren't uncommon in the 19th century.

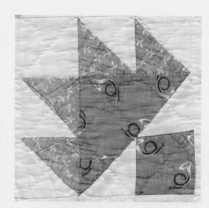

Did you find the French horns? Here they are, and in the quilt above, they're in the seventh red block, counting down from the top.

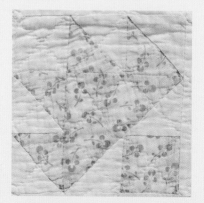

Cream prints weren't likely part of the original quilt. I wonder what color this began as?

Little spare fabric to pull from might be the reason she didn't worry about which direction her stripes ran.

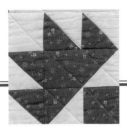

Mix up prints within each color family to give your quilt plenty of interest. Starting with fat eighths rather than yardage will give you the greatest variety, as each one will yield two blocks.

"Men at Work"
Finished quilt: 63½" x 74"
Finished block: 5¼" x 5¼"

Materials

Yardage is based on 42"-wide fabric. Fat eighths are 9" x 21".

Fat eighths or quarter-yard cuts in the following amounts and print colors for blocks:*
   3 brown, 8 indigo blue, 6 burgundy, 5 navy blue, 5 gray, 6 red, 4 black, and 5 pink
4 yards of muslin for blocks
⅝ yard of brown print for binding
4½ yards of fabric for backing
71" x 81" piece of cotton batting
I used an assortment of prints in each color (for example, 3 different browns), but you could use a single print for each color.

Cutting

From *each* fat eighth or quarter yard, cut the following pieces to make 2 blocks:
4 squares, 2⅝" x 2⅝"; cut in half diagonally to yield 8 triangles
2 squares, 2¼" x 2¼"
1 square, 4⅜" x 4⅜"; cut in half diagonally to yield 2 triangles

From the muslin, cut:
14 strips, 5¾" x 42"; crosscut into 84 squares, 5¾" x 5¾"
5 strips, 2¼" x 42"; crosscut into 84 squares, 2¼" x 2¼"
17 strips, 2⅝" x 42"; crosscut into 252 squares, 2⅝" x 2⅝". Cut squares in half diagonally to yield 504 triangles.

From the brown print for binding, cut:
7 strips, 2½" x 42"

Making the Blocks

1. Sew together a muslin 2⅝" triangle and a print 2⅝" triangle to make a half-square-triangle unit. Press the seam allowances toward the print. Repeat to make three more half-square-triangle units using the same print. The half-square-triangle units should measure 2¼" square, including seam allowances.

Make 4.

2. Join the half-square-triangle units in pairs, taking care to orient them correctly as shown.

3. Sew muslin triangles to two adjacent sides of a matching-print 2¼" square. Press the seam allowances toward the print square. Sew the completed unit to a matching-print 4⅜" triangle. Press the seam allowances toward the print. The unit should measure 4" square, including seam allowances.

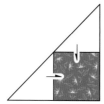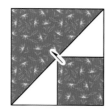

4. Sew the left unit from step 2 to the left edge of the unit from step 3 as shown. Press the seam allowances toward the unit from step 2.

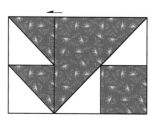

5. Sew a muslin square to the left end of the remaining half-square-triangle units from step 2. Press the seam allowances toward the triangle.

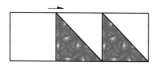

6. Stitch the unit from step 5 to the top edge of the unit from step 4 as shown. Press the seam allowances toward the unit from step 4.

7. Repeat to make a total of 84 blocks, two from each fabric. When all the blocks are pieced, you should have the following totals: 6 brown, 16 indigo blue,

12 burgundy, 10 navy, 10 gray, 12 red, 8 black, and 10 pink blocks. The blocks should measure 5¾" square, including seam allowances.

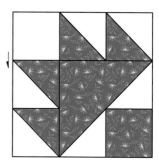

Make 84 total.

Assembling the Quilt Top

1. Referring to the photo on page 19 and the quilt assembly diagram on page 21, arrange the pieced blocks and muslin squares so that the colors run in diagonal rows in the following order, beginning in the upper-right corner: navy, brown, burgundy, black, pink, indigo, red, gray, navy, burgundy, indigo, and brown.

2. Join the blocks in horizontal rows, pressing the seam allowances toward the muslin blocks. Join the rows and press all seam allowances in one direction.

Finishing the Quilt

For more information on finishing your quilt, see ShopMartingale.com/HowtoQuilt.

1. I pieced the backing with a horizontal seam to make better use of the fabric. Layer the backing, batting, and quilt top; baste.

2. Quilt as you wish. The quilt shown was quilted in horizontal rows 1¾" apart and diagonally from left to right 1¼" apart.

3. Bind the quilt using the brown 2½"-wide strips.

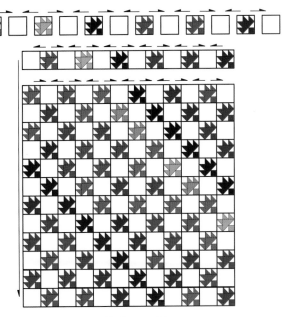

Quilt assembly

Queen-Size Option

To make a queen-size version that is 18 blocks wide and 18 blocks long and finishes at 95" x 95", you'll need the following:

3 additional fat eighths *or* ¾ yard of brown print
1 additional fat eighth *or* quarter-yard cut of gray print
7¾ yards *total* of muslin
¾ yard *total* of brown print for binding
9 yards of fabric for backing
107" x 107" piece of cotton batting

Cutting

From *each* fat eighth or quarter yard, cut the following pieces to make 4 blocks:
8 squares, 2⅝" x 2⅝"; cut in half diagonally to yield 16 triangles
4 squares, 2¼" x 2¼"
2 squares, 4⅜" x 4⅜"; cut in half diagonally to yield 4 triangles

From the muslin, cut:
27 strips, 5¾" x 42"; crosscut into 162 squares, 5¾" x 5¾"
10 strips, 2¼" x 42"; crosscut into 162 squares, 2¼" x 2¼"
33 strips, 2⅝" x 42"; crosscut into 486 squares, 2⅝" x 2⅝". Cut squares in half diagonally to yield 972 triangles.

From the brown print for binding, cut:
9 strips, 2½" x 42"

Referring to the instructions on page 19, piece 162 blocks in the following quantities: 22 brown, 26 indigo, 22 burgundy, 20 navy, 24 gray, 24 red, 18 pink, and 10 black. Arrange the blocks and squares in 18 rows of 18 blocks each in the color order shown in the quilt assembly diagram above, beginning in the upper-right corner. After placing the second row of navy blocks on the lower-left side, continue to place the remaining blocks in this order: red, gray, brown, pink, and black.

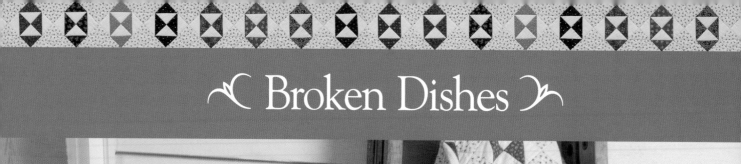

❧ Broken Dishes ❧

Quite often, Broken Dishes quilts are scrappy, and the blocks are set together side by side. What I found so appealing about this version is the setting. First off, each block uses just two fabrics—one colored print plus muslin. And then the blocks are set on point, separated by shirting-print squares, creating the unusual vertical columns of different colors.

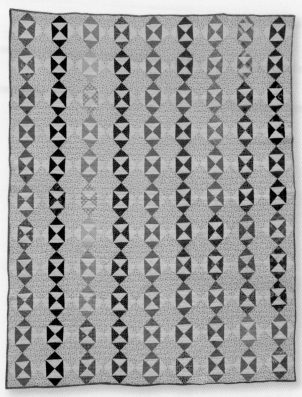

At first glance, each row appears to represent a different color.

A closer look reveals the occasional exception. Is this by choice or by chance changing of the dyes?

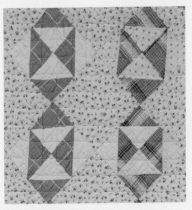

Worried about plaids matching or lining up? She wasn't. She even slipped a shirting print into one block.

Colors mix up more as she gets to the bottom corner. Maybe it's a make-do?

Even when the row is all one color, I prefer to use a scrappy mix of prints. Doing so adds interest to me. If you prefer a more regimented look, substitute a single print in one colorway for all the blocks in a row.

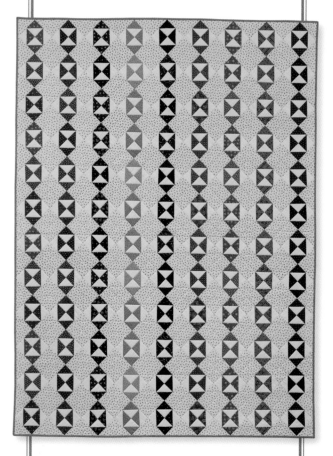

"Broken Dishes"
Finished quilt: 64⅛" x 85⅜"
Finished block: 5" x 5"

Materials

Yardage is based on 42"-wide fabric. Fat eighths are 9" x 21".

3 yards of shirting print for setting squares and triangles
2⅛ yards of muslin for block background
6 fat eighths *each* of assorted blue and brown prints for blocks (12 total)
3 fat eighths *each* of assorted black, burgundy, gray, pink, and red prints for blocks (15 total)
⅔ yard of pink print for binding
5½ yards of fabric for backing
72" x 93" piece of cotton batting

Cutting

From *each* of the assorted prints, cut:
2 strips, 3⅜" x 21"; crosscut into 8 squares, 3⅜" x 3⅜". Cut squares in half diagonally to yield 16 triangles (432 total).

From the muslin, cut:
20 strips, 3⅜" x 42"; crosscut into 216 squares, 3⅜" x 3⅜". Cut squares in half diagonally to yield 432 triangles.

From the shirting print, cut:
13 strips, 5½" x 42"; crosscut into 88 squares, 5½" x 5½"
3 strips, 8½" x 42"; crosscut into 10 squares, 8½" x 8½". Cut squares into quarters diagonally to yield 40 triangles. (You'll have 2 left over.)
2 squares, 4½" x 4½"; cut squares in half diagonally to yield 4 corner triangles

From the pink print for binding, cut:
8 strips, 2½" x 42"

Making the Blocks

1. Sew a print 3⅜" triangle to a muslin 3⅜" triangle. Press the seam allowances toward the print triangle. Repeat to make three more half-square-triangle units using the same print. The units should measure 3" square, including seam allowances.

Make 4.

Assembling the Quilt Top

1. The blocks are joined in diagonal rows, but the colors create vertical columns. Referring to the quilt assembly diagram, arrange the blocks in columns by color, alternating the pieced blocks with the shirting squares. You'll have two rows of blue and brown and one each of the seven remaining colors.

2. Sew the blocks and squares together in diagonal rows, pressing the seam allowances toward the shirting squares. Add the setting triangles at the end of each row as shown.

3. Join the rows, pressing the seam allowances in one direction. Add the corner triangles last.

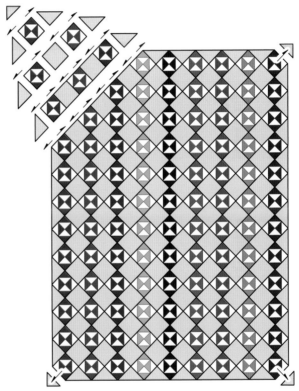

Quilt assembly

2. Sew the half-square-triangle units together in pairs as shown. Pay attention to orientation. Press the seam allowances toward the print triangles.

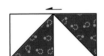

Make 1 of each.

3. Sew the units from step 2 together to complete a block. Repeat with the remaining print and muslin triangles. Make four blocks from each print, 108 blocks total. The blocks should measure 5" square, including seam allowances.

Make 4 from each print,
108 total.

Finishing the Quilt

For more information on finishing your quilt, see ShopMartingale.com/HowtoQuilt.

1. Layer the backing, batting, and quilt top; baste.

2. Quilt as you wish. The quilt shown was quilted in a simple 2½" diagonal grid.

3. Bind the quilt using the pink-print 2½"-wide strips.

❧ Antique Angles ❧

This traditional version of a Thousand Pyramids quilt pattern is perfect for using scraps from your other vintage-inspired quilts. The instructions call for fat eighths of medium and dark prints, but don't hesitate to toss in whatever favorite prints are hanging out in your scrap basket for a rich, interesting quilt in which each fabric begs to be examined closely.

The distribution of red triangles gives a nice sense of movement across the quilt.

Near the bottom row, a handful of medium-tone shirtings work their way into the light positions.

Though most prints are small scale, the occasional larger-scale print does appear from time to time.

Waste not, want not. The quiltmaker pieced together enough to make the black-and-white triangle.

I love shirtings and have built a healthy stash of vintage and reproductions over the years. Though this version uses a single shirting, adding an assortment of scrappy shirtings to the mix would more closely match the original.

"Antique Angles"
Finished quilt: 63" x 76"
Finished block: 4½" x 5½"

Materials

Yardage is based on 42"-wide fabric. Fat eighths are 9" x 21".

46 fat eighths of assorted medium and dark prints for blocks
3½ yards of shirting print for blocks and binding
⅝ yard of dark print for border
4 yards of fabric for backing
70" x 83" piece of cotton batting
45° kaleidoscope ruler or template plastic
Permanent marker for template plastic and fabric marker

Cutting

From *each* of the assorted medium and dark prints, cut:
1 strip, 6½" x 21"

From the shirting print, cut:
15 strips, 6½" x 42"
4 squares, 2½" x 2½"
7 strips, 2½" x 42"

From the dark print for border, cut:
7 strips, 2½" x 42"

Seam Allowance

I used a ¼" seam allowance to sew the triangles together in each of the rows. Because of the more severe tip at the top of a 45° angle, you will then need to sew the rows together with a ½" seam allowance. If you use a ¼" seam allowance to sew the rows together, you'll end up having a ¼" row of cream at the top of the row of dark triangles.

Piecing the Quilt Top

If you're not using a 45° kaleidoscope ruler, first make a plastic template using the triangle pattern on page 31. Lay the template plastic on the pattern and trace the solid lines of the pattern onto the plastic. Cut out the template using a rotary cutter or scissors.

1. Place the 45° kaleidoscope ruler on a medium- or dark-print strip so that the 6½" marking on the ruler is even with the bottom edge of the fabric. Cut four triangles from the strip, flipping the ruler after each cut. Repeat with each of the medium and dark

prints. If using a template, lay the template on the medium- or dark-print strip, aligning the bottom of the template with the edge of the fabric. Using your rotary cutter, carefully cut along both sides of the template to cut a triangle or mark the triangles; rotate the template and cut another triangle. Repeat to cut four triangles per strip.

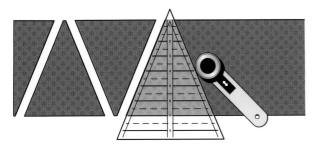

2. In the same manner, cut triangles from the shirting 6½"-wide strips. You should get 12 triangles from each strip.

3. Place a shirting triangle right side down on a print triangle, offsetting the corners so they intersect at the point of the ¼" seam allowance as shown. Stitch and then press the seam allowances toward the print

triangle. Repeat to make 169 pairs of triangles. The remaining muslin and print triangles will be used individually.

 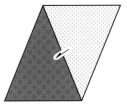

4. Referring to the quilt assembly diagram on page 30, arrange the units from step 3 randomly in horizontal rows with 13 units in each row. Begin row 1 and all odd-numbered rows with a print triangle. Add an individual print triangle to the end of these rows to complete the rows. Begin row 2 and all even-numbered rows with a shirting triangle; add an individual shirting triangle to the end of these rows to complete the rows.

Row 1

Row 2

5. When you're pleased with the arrangement, sew the units into rows. Sew the rows together using a ½" seam allowance.

6. Trim the side edges of the quilt top before adding the border by placing a long ruler along the edge of the quilt, leaving a ¼" seam allowance beyond the points of the triangles. Trim with a rotary cutter.

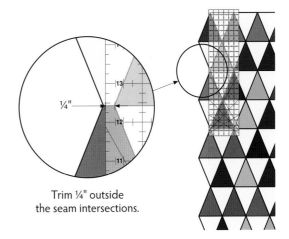

Trim ¼" outside
the seam intersections.

Adding the Border

1. Sew two of the 2½"-wide border strips together end to end to make one long strip. Repeat to make a second strip. Measure the length of the quilt top through the center, and trim the two border strips to the measured length.

2. Sew a border strip to each side of the quilt top. Press the seam allowances toward the border.

3. Cut one 2½"-wide border strip in half and sew one half to the short end of each remaining border strip. Measure the width of the quilt top through the center, not including the side borders, and cut the two strips to the measured length. Sew a shirting 2½" square to each end of both strips, pressing the seam allowances toward the strips.

4. Sew the border strips to the top and bottom of the quilt top. Press the seam allowances toward the border strips.

Finishing the Quilt

For more information on finishing your quilt, see ShopMartingale.com/HowtoQuilt.

1. I pieced the backing with a horizontal seam to make the best use of the fabric. Layer the backing, batting, and quilt top; baste.

2. Quilt as you wish. The quilt shown was machine quilted in parallel diagonal lines running from the upper right to the lower left and spaced 1" apart.

3. Bind the quilt using the shirting 2½"-wide strips.

Re-creating the Past

I always use cotton batting when reproducing an antique quilt, because that's the type of batting used in days gone by. When you wash the new quilt, the batting will shrink just a bit to help create the slightly crinkled look of an antique.

Quilt assembly

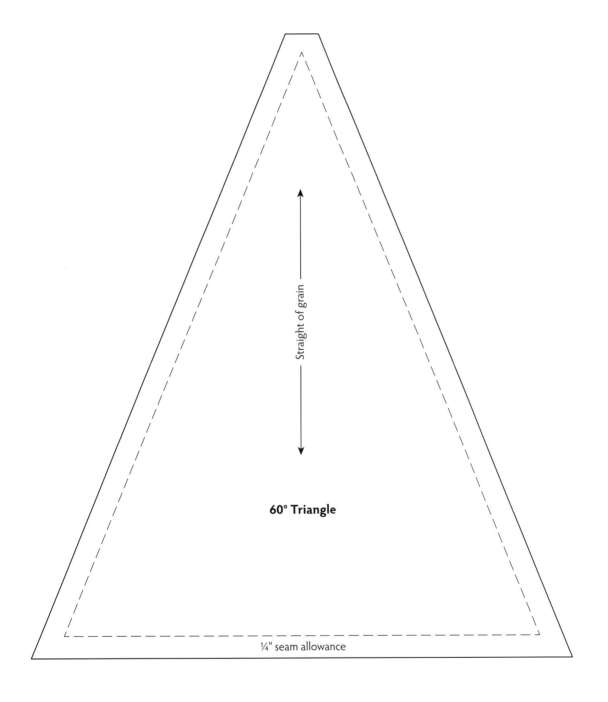

Straight of grain

60° Triangle

¼" seam allowance

Bordered Stars

For this quilt, I changed the original color scheme to make a quilt that was a little less exuberant than the antique, which featured so much double pink fabric. Whether you're a fan of pink or of a more subdued palette, give this quilt a try. The medallion setting with wide expanses of plain borders lets you turn 7″ Sawtooth Star blocks into a large quilt in a jiffy.

Wide, solid borders are excellent spaces for showing off your quilting and cross-hatching skills.

Polka-dot prints look as festive now as they did way back when.

Every which way seemed to be the quiltmaker's plan for stripes on this block.

Was thriftiness the driving factor behind this multi-seamed scrappy block, or artistic license?

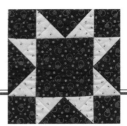

The higher contrast of a light shirting background further emphasizes the two rings of star blocks. Experiment with background colors to get the look you want.

"Bordered Stars"
Finished quilt: 69½" x 69½"
Finished block: 7" x 7"

Materials

Yardage is based on 42"-wide fabric. Fat quarters are 18" x 21".

3⅛ yards of light shirting yardage for center square and borders

¼ yard *each* of 6 light shirting prints for blocks

16 fat quarters of assorted dark prints in indigo, burgundy, black, and pink for blocks

⅝ yard of burgundy print for binding

4½ yards of fabric for backing

82" x 82" piece of cotton batting

Cutting

From the light shirting yardage, cut:
2 strips, 10½" x 69½"
2 strips, 10½" x 49½"
2 strips, 7½" x 35½"
2 strips, 7½" x 21½"
1 square, 7½" x 7½"

From *4* of the light shirting prints, cut:
3 strips, 2¼" x 42"; crosscut into 40 squares, 2¼" x 2¼" (160 total)

From *2* of the light shirting prints, cut:
3 strips, 2¼" x 42"; crosscut into 48 squares, 2¼" x 2¼" (96 total)

From *each* of the 16 fat quarters of dark prints, cut:
1 strip, 4" x 21"; crosscut into 2 squares, 4" x 4" (32 total)
2 strips, 2¼" x 21"; crosscut into 8 rectangles, 2¼" x 4" (128 total)
1 strip, 2¼" x 21"; crosscut into 8 squares, 2¼" x 2¼" (128 total)

From the burgundy print for binding, cut:
7 strips, 2½" x 42"

Re-creating the Past

Shirting is another name for finely woven white cotton fabric with a small-scale print. Defined as fabric used to make men's shirts, it's often used to describe reproduction quilt fabrics that feature small black, brown, or red prints on white.

Making the Blocks

1. Draw a diagonal line from corner to corner on the wrong side of eight matching light-shirting 2¼" squares.

2. Place a marked shirting 2¼" square on one end of a dark 2¼" x 4" rectangle with right sides together. Stitch directly on the line; trim away the excess fabric, leaving a ¼" seam allowance. Press the seam allowances toward the light shirting.

3. In the same manner, place a second marked shirting square at the opposite end of the dark 2¼" x 4" rectangle. Pay attention to the orientation of the line. Sew directly on the line, trim as before, and press the seam allowances toward the light shirting. Repeat to make four matching flying-geese units.

Make 4.

4. Lay out four flying-geese units, four matching dark 2¼" squares, and one dark 4" square in three horizontal rows. Join the units into rows. Join the rows to make a Sawtooth Star block. Press the seam allowances as indicated by the arrows. The block should measure 7½" x 7½". Repeat to make a total of 32 Sawtooth Star blocks.

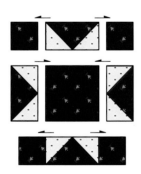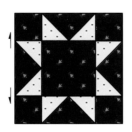

Make 32.

Assembling the Quilt Top

Refer to the quilt assembly diagram on page 36 for these steps.

1. Lay out eight Sawtooth Star blocks and the beige-shirting 7½" square in three horizontal rows.

2. Sew together the blocks in each row. Press the seam allowances in opposite directions from row to row. Sew the rows together. Press. The quilt center should measure 21½" x 21½".

3. Sew the shirting 7½" x 21½" border strips to the left and right sides of the quilt center. Press the seam allowances toward the border strips. Sew the shirting 7½" x 35½" border strips to the top and bottom of the quilt top. Press the seam allowances toward the border strips. The quilt should now measure 35½" x 35½".

4. Join five Sawtooth Star blocks to make a pieced side border. Press the seam allowances in one direction. Repeat to make a second pieced side border.

5. Join seven Sawtooth Star blocks to make a pieced top border. Press the seam allowances in one direction. Repeat to make a second pieced bottom border.

6. Sew the side pieced borders to the quilt top first, then add the top and bottom pieced borders. Press the seam allowances toward the shirting borders.

7. Sew the shirting 10½" x 49½" strips to the left and right sides of the quilt top. Press the seam allowances toward the shirting. Sew the shirting 10½" x 69½" strips to the top and bottom of the quilt top. Press the seam allowances toward the shirting.

Finishing the Quilt

For more information on finishing your quilt, see ShopMartingale.com/HowtoQuilt.

1. Layer the backing, batting, and quilt top; baste.

2. Quilt as you wish. The quilt shown was quilted in a 1" diagonal grid.

3. Bind the quilt using the burgundy 2½"-wide strips.

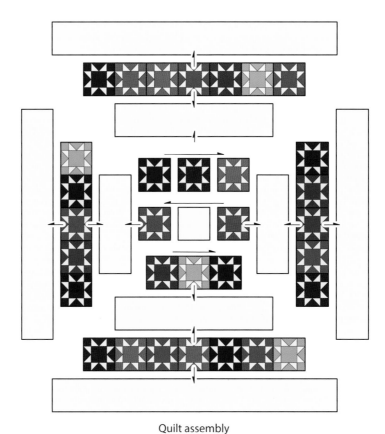

Quilt assembly

Rickrack

Squares of blue, black, indigo, and double pink—all commonly used colors in the late 1800s—are paired with light shirting prints to create the illusion of diagonal rows. In reality, this quilt is pieced in vertical columns that are offset to make the jagged diagonal line. Starting with pieced strip sets makes this quilt easy to assemble and a clever way to showcase simple squares!

For the period in which it was made, I'm in awe of the quiltmaker's ability to see how the pattern would come together.

Twice in the antique quilt, it appears the light/dark alternating-rows pattern is broken.

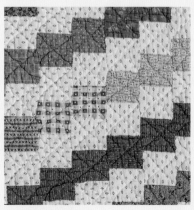

With such a variety of colorful prints, were they cut from old clothing or from swaps with other quilters?

Some sections have more repetition of a single print.

Keeping pieces organized as you sew is the key. Use plastic bags or binder clips to keep like segments together. Work one row at a time. As you complete each row, join it to the adjacent row so you can spot any placement errors at once.

"Rickrack"
Finished quilt: 68" x 78½"
Finished block: 2¼" x 2¼"

Materials

Yardage is based on 42"-wide fabric. Fat quarters are 18" x 21".

1 fat quarter *each* of 20 assorted medium and dark prints for blocks
4 yards of shirting print for blocks and binding
4⅓ yards of fabric for backing
71" x 81" piece of cotton batting

Cutting

From the shirting print, cut:
44 strips, 2¾" x 42", crosscut into:
    77 strips, 2¾" x 21"
    44 squares, 2¾" x 2¾"
    15 rectangles, 1⅝" x 2¾"
7 strips, 2½" x 42"

For the fat quarters, follow the table below:
Number the fat quarters from 1 to 20 in the order you wish them to appear in the quilt from top left to bottom. Refer to the table to cut the required number of pieces from *each* fat quarter.

Fabric number	2¾" x 21" strips	2¾" x 2¾" squares	1⅝" x 2¾" rectangles
1	1	7	2
2	3	2	2
3	2	4	2
4	1	5	2
5	3	0	1
6	3	10	2
7	4	0	1
8	4	4	1
9	5	0	0
10	5	0	0
11	5	0	0
12	5	0	0
13	5	0	0
14	5	0	0
15	5	0	0
16	5	0	0
17	5	2	0
18	5	2	0
19	3	6	1
20	3	2	1

Making the Blocks

Read all instructions before sewing. The fabrics form diagonal stripes across the quilt, but the quilt top is constructed in vertical rows. The rows are made up of strip sets plus individual squares and rectangles that are added to the top and bottom to complete the rows.

Sew the medium- and dark-print strips and shirting strips into strip sets in the combinations listed below. All of the strip sets use two shirting strips except the fabric #2 set, which uses only one. Cut the strip sets into 2¾"-wide segments as indicated.

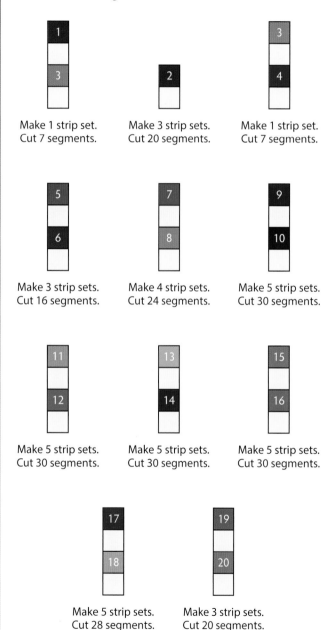

Make 1 strip set.
Cut 7 segments.

Make 3 strip sets.
Cut 20 segments.

Make 1 strip set.
Cut 7 segments.

Make 3 strip sets.
Cut 16 segments.

Make 4 strip sets.
Cut 24 segments.

Make 5 strip sets.
Cut 30 segments.

Make 5 strip sets.
Cut 30 segments.

Make 5 strip sets.
Cut 30 segments.

Make 5 strip sets.
Cut 30 segments.

Make 5 strip sets.
Cut 28 segments.

Make 3 strip sets.
Cut 20 segments.

Assembling the Quilt Top

Odd-numbered rows begin with a rectangle and even-numbered rows begin with a square. Working on a design wall will make it easier to help keep your pieces organized.

1. Arrange the units in vertical rows, beginning in the upper-left corner of the quilt top. Place a 1⅝" x 2¾" rectangle of fabric #1 followed by a shirting-print 2¾" square.

2. Continue down the first vertical column with fabrics #2 through #18, placing strip-set segments in order, and orienting each one so that there is a shirting-print square between each dark-print square. End with a square of fabric #18.

3. Referring to the assembly diagram on page 41, continue to arrange the vertical columns in order so that the colors form diagonal stripes across the quilt. Add colors 19 and 20 across the bottom, and then repeat colors 2, 1, 3, 6, and 5 in the bottom-right corner. Add individual squares and rectangles as needed to complete the top and bottom of each column.

4. Sew the units together into columns, pressing the seam allowances toward the dark prints. Sew the columns together to complete the quilt top.

Finishing the Quilt

For more information on finishing your quilt, see ShopMartingale.com/HowtoQuilt.

1. Layer the backing, batting, and quilt top; baste.
2. Quilt as you wish. The quilt shown was quilted with parallel diagonal lines running from the upper left to the lower right and spaced 1" apart.
3. Bind the quilt using the shirting 2½"-wide strips.

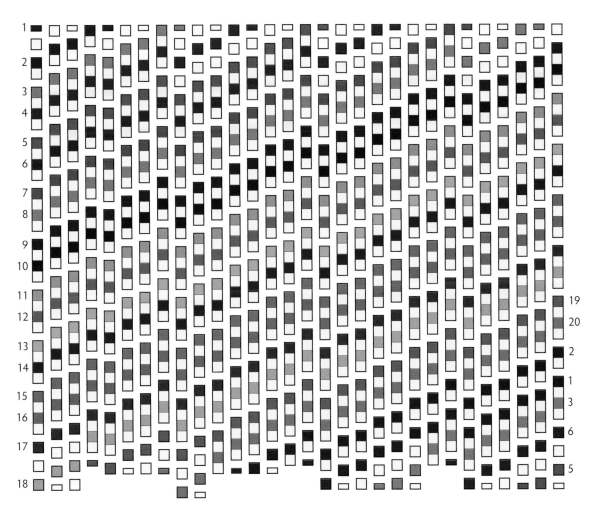

Quilt assembly
Numbers along left and right edges refer to the assigned color numbers.

Indigo and white is a classic color combination from the past that is just as well loved today. In these traditional Martha Washington Star blocks, sparkling white stars on a blue background each feature a small white pinwheel in the center. Look closely and you'll see that some pinwheels turn one way while a few turn the other way.

The surprise addition of red in the outer rows intrigues me.

A colorful plaid in one corner block nearly overwhelms the pinwheel and star altogether.

Not enough medium blue to complete the block? Make do with light blue.

What to do when the backing is too narrow for the top? Lop off one edge of the row to make it work.

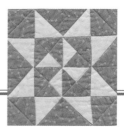

Materials

Yardage is based on 42"-wide fabric. Fat quarters are 18" x 21".

1 fat quarter *each* of 21 assorted blue prints for blocks*
2⅝ yards of shirting print for setting squares
2 yards of muslin for blocks
⅔ yard of blue print for binding
5 yards of fabric for backing
80" x 80" piece of cotton batting

*Each fat quarter yields two blocks.

Cutting

From the muslin, cut:
21 strips, 2½" x 42"; crosscut into 328 squares,
   2½" x 2½"
4 strips, 3¼" x 42"; crosscut into 41 squares,
   3¼" x 3¼". Cut squares into quarters diagonally to
   yield 164 quarter-square triangles.

From the shirting print, cut:
10 strips, 8½" x 42"; crosscut into 40 squares,
   8½" x 8½"

From *each* of the assorted blue prints, cut:
1 strip, 2½" x 21"; crosscut into 8 squares, 2½" x 2½"
   (168 total)
1 strip, 4½" x 21"; crosscut into 8 rectangles,
   2½" x 4½" (168 total)
1 strip, 2⅞" x 21"; crosscut into 4 squares, 2⅞" x 2⅞"
   Cut squares in half diagonally to yield
   8 triangles (168 total)*
2 squares, 3¼" x 3¼"; cut squares into quarters
   diagonally to yield 8 quarter-square triangles*

From the blue print for binding, cut:
8 strips, 2½" x 42"

*Keep the half-square and quarter-square triangles separate to avoid confusing them, as their sizes are similar.

Though I was captivated by the addition of one off-color row, I opted to remake my version sans red in a true scrappy blue-and-muslin palette for the blocks, with a single shirting for the setting squares.

"Under the Stars"
Finished quilt: 72½" x 72½"
Finished block: 8" x 8"

Re-creating the Past

Be very careful when washing quilt fabric and your finished quilt. I wash mine only in Ivory Clear or Orvus Paste, and I do not use detergent, as it can cause colors to fade and can be harsh on your quilts.

Making the Blocks

Use a single blue print for each block. You have cut enough pieces to make 42 blocks, but only 41 are needed.

1. Place a blue quarter-square triangle right sides together with a muslin quarter-square triangle, making sure the triangles are oriented correctly. Sew the triangles together and press the seam allowances toward the blue triangle. Repeat to make a total of four units using the same blue fabric.

Make 4.

Spinning Pinwheels

To make construction easier, I wrote these instructions so that all the pinwheels spin in the same direction. In the quilt shown on page 44, however, the pinwheels in some of the blocks spin in the opposite direction. If you wish to vary the direction of your pinwheels, simply reverse the positions of the quarter-square triangles in step 1.

2. Sew a matching blue half-square triangle to each unit from step 1 as shown. Press the seam allowances toward the larger blue triangle.

Make 4.

3. Join the units from step 2 in pairs, and then join the pairs to complete the center of the Star block.

Size It Up

You can easily enlarge this pattern to a 98" x 98" queen-size quilt by making 20 additional pieced blocks (61 total) and cutting 20 additional shirting squares (60 total). You'll need the following materials:

1 fat quarter *each* of 31 assorted blue prints for blocks
3¾ yards of shirting print for setting squares
3 yards of blue print for border and binding
2¾ yards of muslin for blocks
9 yards of fabric for backing
106" x 106" piece of cotton batting

Follow the "Making the Block" instructions to piece 61 blocks. Arrange the pieced blocks and shirting blocks in 11 rows of 11 blocks each. Sew the blocks together into rows, and then join the rows. Use the blue print to make and add a 5"-wide border to all four sides.

4. Lightly draw a diagonal line on the wrong side of a muslin 2½" square. Place the marked square right sides together on one end of a blue 2½" x 4½" rectangle as shown. Stitch on the marked line. Flip the triangle toward the corner and press. Lift the triangle and trim the excess fabric, leaving a ¼" seam allowance. Layer and stitch a square to the opposite corner of the rectangle. Press and trim as before. Repeat to make a total of four units.

Make 4.

Press First

I've found that if I flip the triangle open and press before trimming, the rectangle will not press out of shape as easily.

5. Add a matching blue 2½" square to each end of two units from step 4. Press the seam allowances toward the squares.

Make 2.

6. Add a unit from step 4 to each side of the block center from step 3. Press the seam allowances toward the block center.

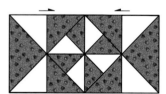

7. Add the units from step 5 to the top and bottom of the unit from step 6 to complete the block. Repeat to make a total of 41 blocks.

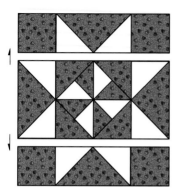

Make 41.

Assembling the Quilt Top

1. Referring to the quilt assembly diagram, arrange the 41 pieced blocks and the 40 shirting squares in nine rows of nine blocks each. Sew the blocks together in rows, pressing the seam allowances toward the pieced blocks.

2. Sew the rows together and press all seam allowances in one direction.

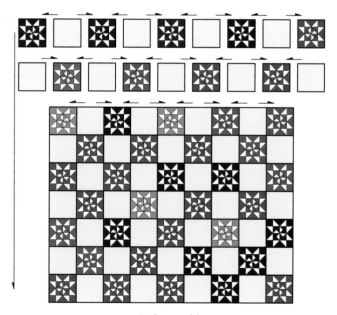

Quilt assembly

Finishing the Quilt

For more information on finishing your quilt, see ShopMartingale.com/HowtoQuilt.

1. Layer the backing, batting, and quilt top; baste.

2. Quilt as you wish. In the quilt shown, each block was quilted in a 2"-wide grid horizontally and vertically and then diagonally in each direction.

3. Bind the quilt using the blue 2½"-wide strips.

Flying North

According to renowned, late quiltmaker Judy Hopkins, the Shoofly variation block used in this quilt is called Cut the Corners. Whatever its name, I think it's the intricate horizontal zigzag setting that really revs up this quilt design. Notice that to create the chevron effect, you need half blocks to start and end alternate rows, which makes this quilt a little more challenging than others. But it's well worth the effort!

The antique version I purchased is an unquilted top.

Some blocks appear to be crosses, not squares when set into the dark background. Dark-blue triangles along the outer edges blend in with adjacent background fabric.

Blocks with high-contrast fabrics make it easier to see the individual elements that make up the block.

A busy plaid blurs the lines of the flying geese because the color values are similar.

The orientation of my quilt is taller and more narrow, but I kept the half blocks on the quilt sides, as in the original. Doing so makes a clean edge with complete blocks at the top of the quilt.

"Flying North"
Finished quilt: 66⅞" x 81¾"
Finished block: 10½" x 10½"

Materials

Yardage is based on 42"-wide fabric. Fat eighths are 9" x 21".

11 fat eighths of assorted light prints for blocks (each print will yield 2 blocks)
22 fat eighths of assorted dark prints for blocks (each print will be used twice)
4 yards of navy print for background
⅔ yard of light print for binding
5 yards of fabric for backing
74" x 89" piece of cotton batting

Cutting

From *each* of the assorted light prints:
1 strip, 4⅜" x 21"; crosscut into 4 squares, 4⅜" x 4⅜".
    Cut squares in half diagonally to yield 8 triangles
    (88 total).
2 strips, 2¼" x 2¼"; crosscut into 32 squares,
    2¼" x 2¼" (352 total)

From *each* of the assorted dark prints, cut:
1 strip, 4⅜" x 21"; crosscut into:
    2 squares, 4⅜" x 4⅜"; cut in half diagonally to yield
    4 triangles (88 total)
1 square, 4" x 4" (22 total)
1 strip, 4" x 21"; crosscut into 8 rectangles, 2¼" x 4"
    (176 total)

From the navy print, cut:
8 strips, 4" x 42"
5 strips, 16¼" x 42"; crosscut into 9 squares,
    16¼" x 16¼". Cut squares into quarters diagonally
    to yield 36 triangles (2 will be left over).

From the light print for binding, cut:
8 strips, 2½" x 42"

Making the Blocks

For each block, use one light print and two different dark prints—one for the flying-geese units and one for the triangle squares and center square. It's easiest to audition the fabrics first and decide on all the combinations before you begin assembling the blocks.

1. Lightly draw a diagonal line on the wrong side of a light 2¼" square. Place the marked square right sides together on one end of a dark 2¼" x 4" rectangle as shown. Stitch on the marked line. Flip the triangle toward the corner and press. Lift the triangle and trim the excess fabric, leaving a ¼" seam allowance. Layer and stitch a light square to the opposite corner of the rectangle. Press and trim as before. Repeat to make a total of eight matching flying-geese units.

Make 8.

> **Press First!**
>
> I find that by pressing the triangle before trimming, the rectangle doesn't press out of shape as easily.

2. With right sides facing, sew together a light 4⅜" triangle and a dark 4⅜" triangle (different from the dark print used in step 1). Press the seam allowances toward the dark triangle. The unit should measure 4" square. Repeat to make a total of four matching triangle squares.

Make 4.

3. Arrange the eight matching flying-geese units, the four matching triangle squares, and a dark-print 4" square that matches the triangle squares, as shown. Join the units into rows, pressing the seam allowances toward the triangle squares and the center square. Join the rows to complete the block. Press the seam allowances toward the block center. The blocks should measure 11", including seam allowances. Repeat to make 22 blocks.

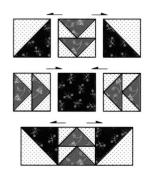 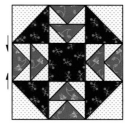

Make 22.

Assembling the Quilt Top

1. Referring to the assembly diagram below, arrange the blocks and setting triangles in horizontal rows. Sew the blocks and setting triangles together, pressing the seam allowances toward the setting pieces.
2. Trim the second and fourth rows, leaving a ¼" seam allowance outside the seam intersections.

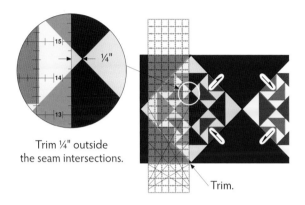

Trim ¼" outside
the seam intersections.

Trim.

3. Join the rows to complete the quilt center. Press all seam allowances in one direction.

Adding the Border

1. Sew the navy 4" x 42" strips in pairs end to end to make four long border strips. Measure the length of the quilt top through the center, and trim the two strips to this length. Sew them to the sides of the quilt top, pressing the seam allowances toward the border.
2. Measure the width of the quilt top through the center, and trim the remaining strips to this length. Sew them to the top and bottom of the quilt top, pressing the seam allowances toward the border.

Finishing the Quilt

For more information on finishing your quilt, go to ShopMartingale.com/HowtoQuilt.

1. Layer the backing, batting, and quilt top; baste.
2. Quilt as you wish. The quilt shown was machine quilted in a 1¾" diagonal grid.
3. Bind the quilt using the light-print 2½"-wide strips.

Adding borders

Star Crossing

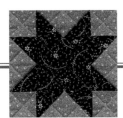

"Star Crossing" is the only quilt in this book that doesn't have an antique mate. But it was based on popular traits of the era—Sawtooth Star blocks, a light shirting print for the background, and a classic double-pink background for the stars that form the X through the center of the quilt. Imagine how this quilt would look if you reversed the placement of the background fabrics or used a light blue in place of the cream prints. Go ahead—make this truly your own!

"Star Crossing"
Finished quilt: 74½" x 74½"
Finished block: 6" x 6"

Materials

Yardage is based on 42"-wide fabric. Fat eighths are 9" x 21".

3⅛ yards of light shirting yardage for setting squares and border

1½ yards of pink print for blocks and binding

½ yard *each* of 3 light shirting prints for blocks

30 fat eighths of assorted dark prints for blocks

4⅞ yards of fabric for backing*

87" x 87" piece of cotton batting

*If your fabric is less than 42" wide, you may need three lengths of fabric for backing, or a total of 7¼ yards.

Cutting

From the light shirting yardage, cut:
10 strips, 6½" x 42; crosscut into 60 squares, 6½" x 6½"
8 strips, 4½" x 42"

From the pink print, cut:
13 strips, 2" x 42"; crosscut into:
    84 rectangles, 2" x 3½"
    84 squares, 2" x 2"
8 strips, 2½" x 42"

From *2* of the light shirting prints, cut:
8 strips, 2" x 42"; crosscut into:
    52 rectangles, 2" x 3½" (104 total)
    52 squares, 2" x 2" (104 total)

From *1* of the light shirting prints, cut:
8 strips, 2" x 42"; crosscut into:
    56 rectangles, 2" x 3½"
    56 squares, 2" x 2"

From *29* of the dark prints, cut:
1 strip, 3½" x 42"; crosscut into 2 squares, 3½" x 3½" (58 total)
2 strips, 2" x 42"; crosscut into 16 squares, 2" x 2" (464 total)

From the remaining dark print, cut:
2 strips, 2" x 21"; crosscut into 20 squares, 2" x 2"
1 strip, 4" x 21"; crosscut into:
    3 squares, 3½" x 3½"
    4 squares, 2" x 2"

Making the Blocks

1. Draw a diagonal line from corner to corner on the wrong side of eight matching dark 2" squares.

2. Place a marked dark 2" square on one end of a light 2" x 3½" rectangle with right sides together. Stitch directly on the line; trim away the excess fabric, leaving a ¼" seam allowance. Press the seam allowances toward the dark print.

3. In the same manner, place a second marked dark 2" square at the opposite end of the light 2" x 3½" rectangle, orienting the marked line as shown. Sew directly on the line, trim as before, and press the seam allowances toward the dark triangle. Repeat to make four flying-geese units using the same light and dark prints.

Make 4.

4. Lay out four flying-geese units, four matching light 2" squares, and one matching dark 3½" square in three horizontal rows. Join the units into rows, and then join the rows to make a Sawtooth Star block. Press the seam allowances as indicated by the arrows. The block should measure 6½" x 6½". Repeat to make a total of 40 Sawtooth Star blocks, using one light-shirting print and one dark print per block.

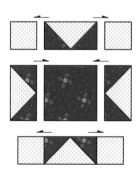

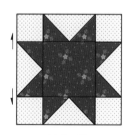

Make 40.

5. Repeat to make 21 Sawtooth Star blocks using the pink print for background instead of the light shirting. The blocks should measure 6½" x 6½".

Make 21.

Assembling the Quilt Top

1. Referring to the quilt assembly diagram on page 55, lay out the 40 light-background Sawtooth Star blocks, the 60 shirting 6½" squares, and the 20 pink-background Sawtooth Star blocks to form an X.

2. Sew the blocks and squares together in each row. Press the seam allowances toward the shirting squares.

3. Join the rows to complete the quilt center. Press all seam allowances in one direction.

Adding the Border

1. Sew the shirting 4½" x 42" strips in pairs end to end with a diagonal seam to make four long border strips. Measure the length of the quilt top through the center, and trim two of the strips to this length. Sew them to opposite sides of the quilt top, pressing the seam allowances toward the border.

2. Measure the width of the quilt top through the center, and trim the two remaining border strips to this length. Sew them to the top and bottom of the quilt top, pressing the seam allowances toward the border.

Finishing the Quilt

For more information on finishing your quilt, see ShopMartingale.com/HowtoQuilt.

1. Layer the backing, batting, and quilt top; baste.
2. Quilt as you wish. The quilt shown was quilted in a 1"-wide diagonal grid.
3. Bind the quilt using the pink 2½"-wide strips.

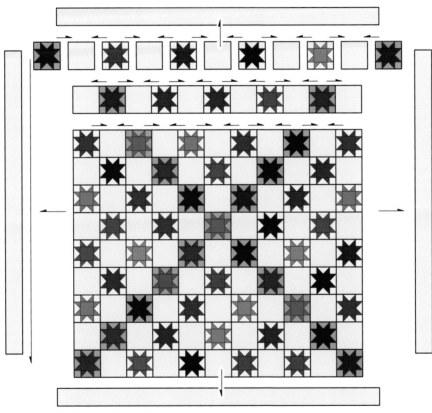

Quilt assembly

Nine Patch Road

What looks like a giant checkerboard of a quilt is actually made using basic Nine Patch blocks. You'll need 85 blocks with dark corners and 84 with light corners. Yes, that's a lot of blocks, but they're a cinch to make, and when the result is this delightful, what are you waiting for?

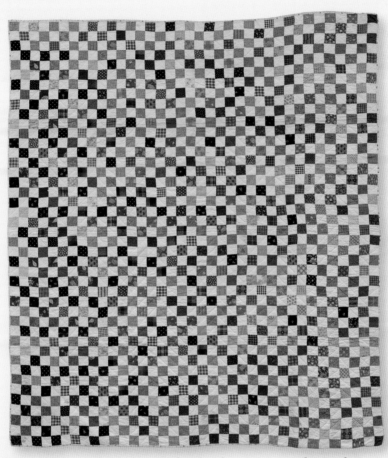

The variety of fabrics used makes this pattern a perfect one for swapping small bits of your stash with quilting friends.

Because several plaids and checks appear often, I wonder if some might have come from old garments.

Though most of the prints are quite small, a few larger-scale motifs are scattered throughout.

It looks to me as if the quiltmaker fussy cut some of her pieces, like this centered stripe.

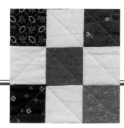

Strip piecing speeds up the process of making the Nine Patch blocks. But if you love a scrappier look (and have a hefty stash of scraps), imagine making this a charm quilt where no print is used twice!

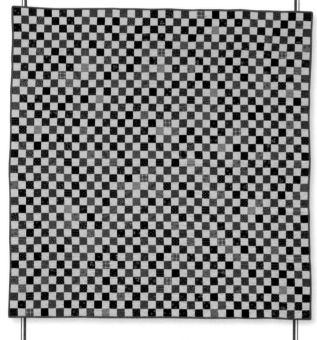

"Nine Patch Road"
Finished quilt: 68¾" x 68¾"
Finished block: 5¼" x 5¼"

Materials

Yardage is based on 42"-wide fabric. Fat eighths are 9" x 21".

46 fat eighths of assorted medium and dark prints for blocks
3¼ yards of muslin for blocks
⅝ yard of brown plaid for binding
4½ yards of fabric for backing
72" x 72" piece of cotton batting

Cutting

From *each* of the fat eighths, cut:
2 strips, 2¼" x 21"; crosscut each into 2 strips, 2¼" x 10½"

From *4* of the fat eighths, cut:
1 strip, 2¼" x 21"; crosscut into 2 strips, 2¼" x 10½"

From the muslin, cut:
48 strips, 2¼" x 42"; crosscut into 4 strips, 2¼" x 10½"

From the brown plaid for binding, cut:
7 strips, 2½" x 42"

Making the Blocks

1. Randomly select two medium- or dark-print strips. Sew one strip to each side of a muslin strip to make a strip sets. Press the seam allowances toward the print strips. Repeat to make 64 strip sets. Cut four 2¼" segments from each strip set.

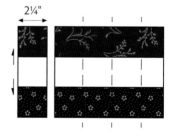

Make 64 strip sets.
Cut 256 segments.

2. In the same manner, sew a muslin strip to each side of a medium- or dark-print strip. Press the seam

allowances toward the print strip. Repeat to make 64 strip sets. Cut four 2¼" segments from each strip set.

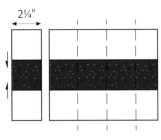

Make 64 strip sets.
Cut 256 segments.

3. Randomly arrange the segments into Nine Patch blocks as shown. Sew the segments together to make 85 A blocks with dark corners and 84 B blocks with light corners. On the A blocks, press the seam allowances toward the top and bottom of the block. On the B blocks, press the seam allowances toward the center segment. This will make it easier to join the blocks into rows. The blocks should measure 5¾" square, including seam allowances.

Block A
Make 85.

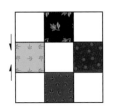

Block B
Make 84.

Assembling the Quilt Top

1. Arrange the quilt top in 13 horizontal rows of 13 blocks per row. Start row 1 with an A block and row 2 with a B block. Continue to place the blocks, alternating A and B blocks across the rows. You may need to rotate some blocks so that seam allowances will nestle together with the adjacent block.

2. Sew the blocks together into rows, pressing the seam allowances in opposite directions from row to row.

3. Sew the rows together. Press all seam allowances in one direction.

Finishing the Quilt

For more information on finishing your quilt, see ShopMartingale.com/HowtoQuilt.

1. Layer the backing, batting, and quilt top; baste.

2. Quilt as you wish. I studied the quilting on the antique quilt and discovered it's quilted in a crosshatch design across the entire quilt. The lines run diagonally through the corners of each square.

3. Bind the quilt using the brown-plaid 2½"-wide strips.

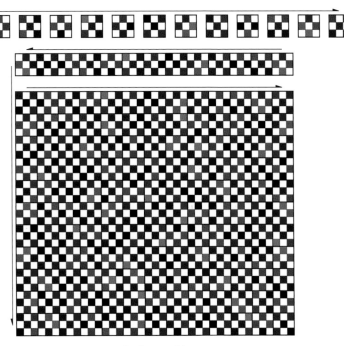

Quilt assembly

❧ Sister's Choice ❧

A variety of blue prints gets an extra dash of interest by also mixing in black prints when sewing the Sister's Choice blocks and Sawtooth border for this quilt. When the blocks are set together with large half-square-triangle units, this quilt really comes alive. The maker who designed this dynamic quilt may have simply been extending the size by adding the split setting squares, but whatever her motive, she came up with a gem!

*The lower-right corner block must have come up a bit short,
so the quiltmaker pieced in extra bits on two sides.*

*A Nine Patch center with star
points at the corners is the pattern
of a Sister's Choice block.*

*Twice in the quilt top, the pattern is
broken. Here the top two star points
were rotated out of position.*

*And here the rotation problems and
a mix of fabrics make me wonder—
was she teaching someone else to
quilt along with her?*

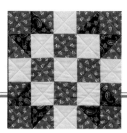

The mysteries antique quilts hold intrigue me. I didn't include the misshaped blocks of the original, but did add my own twist to this remake by rotating the lower-right corner one turn out of alignment. A wink to the spirit of the original!

"Sister's Choice"
Finished quilt: 64½" x 74½"
Finished block: 10" x 10"

Materials

Yardage is based on 42"-wide fabric. Fat quarters are 18" x 21".

2⅞ yards of muslin for blocks and border

1⅓ yards of blue print for large triangles

11 fat quarters of assorted indigo prints for blocks

7 fat quarters of assorted black prints for blocks

⅔ yard of indigo print for binding

4⅞ yards of fabric for backing

77" x 87" piece of cotton batting

Cutting

From the muslin, cut:

4 strips, 10⅞" x 42"; crosscut into 11 squares, 10⅞" x 10⅞".* Cut squares in half diagonally to yield 22 triangles. (You'll have 1 left over.)

13 strips, 2½" x 42"; crosscut into 198 squares, 2½" x 2½"

6 strips, 2⅞" x 42"; crosscut into 77 squares, 2⅞" x 2⅞". Cut squares in half diagonally to yield 134 triangles.

From the blue print, cut:

4 strips, 10⅞" x 42"; crosscut into 11 squares, 10⅞" x 10⅞".* Cut squares in half diagonally to yield 22 triangles. (You'll have 1 left over.)

From *10* of the indigo fat quarters, cut:

2 strips, 2½" x 21"; crosscut into 16 squares, 2½" x 2½" (160 total)

2 strips, 2⅞" x 21"; crosscut into 11 squares, 2⅞" x 2⅞". Cut squares in half diagonally to yield 22 triangles (220 total).

From the remaining indigo fat quarter, cut:

2 strips, 2½" x 21"; crosscut into 16 squares, 2½" x 2½"

2 strips, 2⅞" x 21"; crosscut into 12 squares, 2⅞" x 2⅞". Cut squares in half diagonally to yield 24 triangles. (You'll have 1 left over.)

From *each* of the 7 black prints, cut:

3 strips, 2⅞" x 21"; crosscut into 18 squares, 2⅞" x 2⅞". Cut squares in half diagonally to yield 34 triangles (252 total). (You'll use 176 for blocks and 67 for pieced border. You'll have 9 left over.)

From the indigo print for binding, cut:

8 strips, 2½" x 42"

*If you prefer, cut the muslin and blue square to be 11" instead of 10⅞" for a bit of leeway when assembling the quilt top.

Making the Blocks

You have cut enough pieces to make 22 blocks, but only 21 are needed. Each indigo print is used in two blocks, six black prints are used in three blocks, and one black print is used in four blocks.

1. Sew an indigo 2⅞" triangle to a black 2⅞" triangle along the diagonal to make a half-square-triangle unit. Press the seam allowances toward the black print. The half-square-triangle unit should measure 2½" x 2½". Repeat to make a total of eight half-square-triangle units using the same indigo and black fabrics.

Make 8.

2. Sew five muslin 2½" squares and four indigo 2½" squares (matching indigo used in step 1) to make a Nine Patch block. Press the seam allowances as indicated by the arrows. The block should measure 5" x 5".

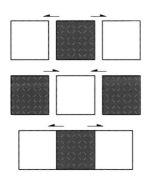 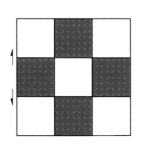

3. Lay out the half-square-triangle units from step 1, the Nine Patch block, four muslin 2½" squares, and four matching indigo 2½" squares as shown. Sew the pieces together to complete the block, pressing the seam allowances as indicated by the arrows. The block should measure 10½" x 10½". Repeat to make a total of 21 blocks. You'll have pieces left over for one block.

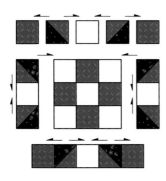 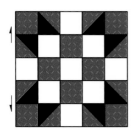

Make 21.

Making the Setting Squares

Sew a blue 10⅞" triangle to a muslin 10⅞" triangle along the diagonal to make a half-square-triangle unit. Press the seam allowances toward the blue print. The pieced unit should measure 10½" x 10½". Repeat to make a total of 21 half-square-triangle units.

Make 21.

Making the Pieced Border

Sew an indigo 2⅞" triangle to a muslin 2⅞" triangle along the diagonal to make a half-square-triangle unit. Press the seam allowances toward the indigo print. The half-square-triangle unit should measure 2½" x 2½". Make a total of 67 half-square-triangle units using the indigo prints and muslin. Repeat to make a total of 67 half-square-triangle units using the black prints and muslin.

Make 67 blue and 67 black.

Assembling the Quilt Top

1. Lay out the 21 blocks and the 21 half-square-triangle units in seven horizontal rows of six blocks each as shown below in the assembly diagram.

2. Sew the blocks and units in each row together. Press the seam allowances in opposite directions from row to row. Sew the rows together. Press the seam allowances in one direction. The center should measure 60½" x 70½".

3. For the top border, sew together 30 half-square-triangle units as shown using the various indigo and black units. Press the seam allowances in one direction. Repeat to make a second border for the bottom of the quilt, noting that the direction of the triangle slant is opposite in the quilt shown.

4. Sew the top and bottom borders onto the quilt top with the white edges of the triangles adjoining the quilt top. Press the seam allowances away from the border.

5. Assemble the side border by sewing 37 half-square-triangle units together as shown using the various indigo and black units. Refer to the quilt assembly diagram, and again note that the triangles slant in opposite directions from one border to the other. Press the seam allowances in one direction. Repeat to make a second border.

6. Sew the side borders onto the quilt top with the white triangles adjoining the quilt top. Press the seam allowances away from the border.

Finishing the Quilt

For more information on finishing your quilt, see ShopMartingale.com/HowtoQuilt.

1. Layer the backing, batting, and quilt top; baste.

2. Quilt as you wish. The quilt shown was quilted 1" diagonal grid.

3. Bind the quilt using the indigo 2½"-wide strips.

Quilt assembly

Double pinks, as they were known in the day, are actually tiny red prints printed over a pink background. Here you can get your fill of pink (and then some!) by using it for setting squares and borders. It makes such a cheerful backdrop to the pieced blocks of much more somber colors. No wonder women of the late 19th century loved it so.

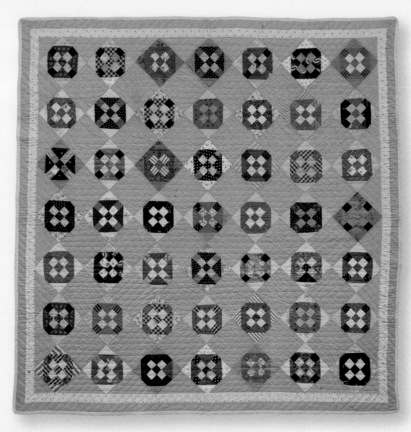

The quilting is done with evenly spaced horizontal lines across the quilt top, and evenly spaced diagonal lines from upper right to lower left.

Don't be afraid to mix red prints into a quilt with double pinks. The burst of color is striking.

Different value placements result in differing looks. High contrast highlights each block element.

The values of the square-in-the-square are so similar here, that the X appears more prominent.

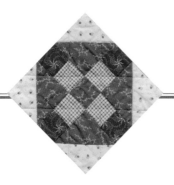

I'm a shoo-in for antique quilts with double pinks. The cheerful look speaks to my heart. And fortunately for quilters today, there are great reproduction prints available that replicate the look.

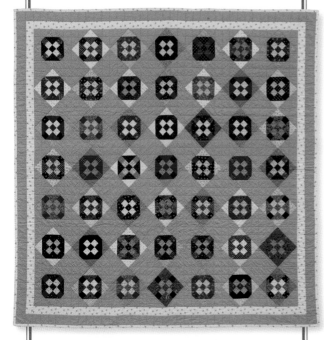

"In the Pink"
Finished quilt: 70⅜" x 70⅜"
Finished block: 6¼" x 6¼"

Materials

Yardage is based on 42"-wide fabric. Fat eighths are 9" x 21".

2⅞ yards of pink print for setting squares, setting triangles, and outer border

2⅝ yards of white-and-black print for inner border and binding

25 fat eighths of assorted dark and medium prints for blocks

20 fat eighths of assorted light prints for blocks

4⅔ yards of fabric for backing

83" x 83" piece of cotton batting

Cutting

From the pink print, cut:

2 strips, 2¾" x 70⅜"

2 strips, 2¾" x 65⅞"

9 strips, 6¾" x 31"; crosscut into 36 squares, 6¾" x 6¾"

1 strip, 5½" x 31"; crosscut into 2 squares, 5½" x 5½". Cut squares in half diagonally to yield 4 triangles.

2 strips, 10¼" x 42"; crosscut into 6 squares, 10¼" x 10¼". Cut squares into quarters diagonally to yield 24 triangles.

From the white-and-black print, cut:

2 strips, 2¼" x 65⅞"

2 strips, 2¼" x 62⅜"

8 strips, 2½" x 42"

From *each* of the medium and dark prints, cut:

1 strip, 3⅜" x 21"; crosscut into 4 squares, 3⅜" x 3⅜". Cut squares in half diagonally to yield 8 triangles (200 total; you'll only use 196)

1 strip, 1¾" x 21"; crosscut into 10 squares, 1¾" x 1¾" (250 total; you'll only use 245)

From *each* of the light prints, cut:

1 strip, 3⅜" x 21"; crosscut into 5 squares, 3⅜" x 3⅜". Cut squares in half diagonally to yield 10 triangles (200 total; you'll only use 196)

1 strip, 1¾" x 21"; crosscut into 10 squares, 1¾" x 1¾" (200 total; you'll only use 196)

Making the Blocks

For one block you'll need four small triangles and one 1¾" square in the same dark or medium print, four small triangles of one light print, four 1¾" squares in a different light print, and four 1¾" squares in another dark or medium print.

1. Sew a dark or medium 3⅜" triangle to a light 3⅜" triangle along the diagonal to make a half-square-triangle unit. Press the seam allowances toward the dark print. The unit should measure 3" x 3". Repeat to make a total of four half-square-triangle units.

Make 4.

2. Join one dark or medium 1¾" square and one light 1¾" square to make a rectangle unit. Press the seam allowances toward the darker print. The rectangle unit should measure 1¾" x 3" including seam allowance. Repeat to make a total of four rectangle units.

Make 4.

3. Lay out the half-square-triangle units from step 1, the rectangle units from step 2, and a dark or medium 1¾" square as shown. Join the units in each row, and then join the rows, pressing the seam allowances as indicated by the arrows. The block should measure 6¾" x 6¾". Repeat to make a total of 49 blocks.

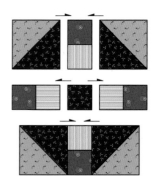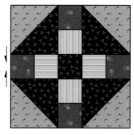

Make 49.

Assembling the Quilt Top

1. Lay out the 49 blocks, the 36 pink 6¾" squares, the 24 pink side setting triangles, and the four corner triangles in 15 diagonal rows.

2. Join the blocks, squares, and triangles in each row. Press the seam allowances toward the pink print. Sew the rows together. Press seam allowances in one direction. The center should measure 62⅜" x 62⅜".

Quilt assembly

Adding the Borders

1. Sew the white-and-black 2¼" x 62⅜" inner-border strips to the sides of the quilt. Press the seam allowances away from the center. Sew the white-and-black 2¼" x 65⅞" inner-border strips to the top and bottom. Press the seam allowances away from the center.

2. Sew the pink 2¾" x 65⅞" outer-border strips to the sides of the quilt. Press the seam allowances toward the pink print. Sew the pink 2¾" x 70⅜" outer-border strips to the top and bottom. Press the seam allowances toward the pink print.

Finishing the Quilt

For more information on finishing your quilt, see ShopMartingale.com/HowtoQuilt.

1. Layer the backing, batting, and quilt top; baste.

2. Quilt as you wish. The featured quilt was quilted with a 1¾"-wide grid.

3. Bind the quilt using the white-and-black 2½"-wide strips.

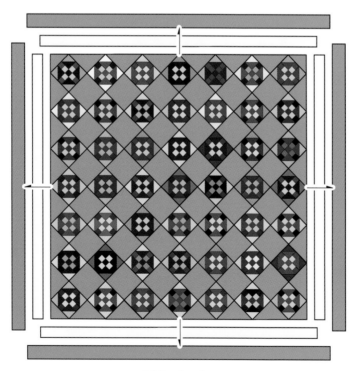

Adding borders

Petite Stars

Tiny white Ohio Stars on colorful backgrounds make this quilt sparkle. Be sure to mix up the variety of prints you use to make this lap-sized quilt interesting to piece and a joy to behold. This is the perfect project to use up your scraps. Each block background requires about a 7" square of fabric.

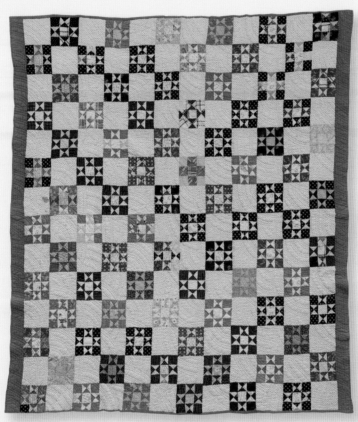

The red borders and binding are actually the backing turned to the front of the quilt. Why?
To stretch the width of the quilt? To make use of every bit of the backing? I wish I knew.

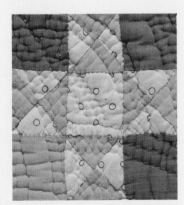

Blocks don't always appear to be from two colors, but unstable dyes might have been the cause.

The light/dark value of this combination makes seeing the star emerge a bit more difficult.

And here the color shifts and placements make the star virtually disappear.

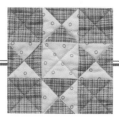

When remaking antique quilt patterns, I like to keep some of the same characteristics of the original. To that end, I add a few blocks with the differing value placements, or rogue fabric centers, to keep the lively spirit.

"Petite Stars"
Finished quilt: 50" x 68"
Finished block: 4½" x 4½"

Materials

Yardage is based on 42"-wide fabric.

3¼ yards *total* of assorted light shirting prints for blocks and setting squares

2¼ yards *total* of assorted red, blue, pink, tan, and gray prints for blocks

⅝ yard of light shirting print for binding

3½ yards of fabric for backing

62" x 80" piece of cotton batting

Cutting

From the assorted shirting prints, cut:

83 matching sets of 2 squares, 2¾" x 2¾", *and* 1 square, 2" x 2"

82 squares, 5" x 5"

From the assorted red, blue, pink, tan, and gray prints, cut:

83 matching sets of 2 squares, 2¾" x 2¾", *and* 4 squares, 2" x 2"

From the shirting print for binding, cut:

7 strips, 2½" x 42"

Making the Blocks

1. Draw diagonal lines in both directions on the wrong side of the assorted shirting 2¾" squares. Place a marked square on an assorted red, blue, pink, tan, or gray 2¾" square, right sides together. Sew ¼" from each side of one line. Cut apart on the unsewn line first, then on the remaining drawn line to form four pieced triangle units. Open and press the seam allowances toward the dark prints. Repeat with matching light and colored squares to complete a set of eight pieced triangles. Make 83 sets total.

Assembling the Quilt Top

1. Arrange the quilt top in 15 horizontal rows of 11 blocks per row. Alternate the placement of blocks and shirting 5" squares.

2. Sew the blocks together into rows, pressing the seam allowances in each row toward the shirting squares.

3. Sew the rows together. Press the seam allowances in one direction.

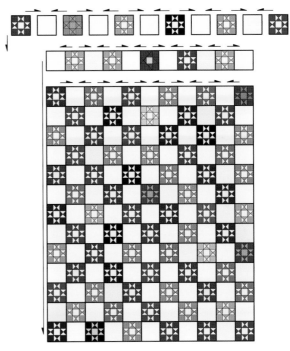

Quilt assembly

2. Sew matching pieced triangles together to make a pieced square. Press the seam allowances as shown. The block should measure 2" x 2". Make 83 sets of four matching units.

Make 83 sets of 4 matching units.

3. Lay out four matching sets from step 2, one matching shirting 2" square, and four matching print 2" squares. Sew the squares into rows; press the seam allowances in opposite directions from row to row. Sew the rows together, pressing the seam allowances away from the block center. The block should measure 5" x 5". Repeat to make 83 blocks total.

Finishing the Quilt

For more information on finishing your quilt, go to ShopMartingale.com/HowtoQuilt.

1. Layer the backing, batting, and quilt top; baste.

2. Quilt as you wish. The quilt shown was quilted in an overall crosshatching pattern. The antique version was quilted in a Baptist fan design.

3. Bind the quilt using the shirting 2½"-wide strips.

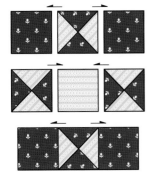 

Make 83.

The unknown maker of this quilt apparently started with a plan to make checkerboard-style blocks. Whether she ran out of pieces large enough or just decided to raid her scrap basket for a wider variety of prints, we can only guess. While most of her 56 blocks have a checkerboard look, only 14 use just two fabrics in true checkerboard style.

I'm captivated by the cheddar blocks in the quilt and the fact that they're placed only around the edges of the quilt. Because cheddar prints were not available at the time I was going to remake this quilt, I didn't make a new version. I often look for reproduction fabrics that follow the integrity of the original version.

A few blocks have decidedly diagonal color placement.

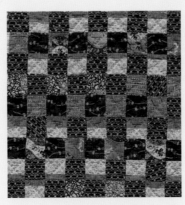

Because of the fabric choices, this block looks as if it is woven in an over-and-under fashion.

This block has a bull's-eye center surrounded by rings of color.

"81-Patch"
Finished quilt: 79¼" x 90½"
Finished block: 11¼" x 11¼"

Materials

Yardage is based on 42"-wide fabric.

10½ yards *total* of assorted pink, orange, brown, cream, blue, green, gold, black, and red prints for blocks
¾ yard of brown stripe for binding
7⅔ yards of fabric for backing
92" x 103" piece of cotton batting

Cutting

From *each of 28* assorted prints, cut:
9 strips, 1¾" x 9" (252 total)

From *all* assorted prints, cut a *total* of:
3402 squares, 1¾" x 1¾"

From the brown stripe for binding, cut:
9 strips, 2½" x 42"

Making the A Blocks

For this quilt, you'll be making two sets of blocks, 14 two-fabric blocks (A blocks) and 42 scrappy blocks (B blocks).

1. Select nine 1¾" x 9" strips: five of one print and four of another. Join the strips, alternating them as shown, to make a strip set. Press the seam allowances toward the darker print. Cut the strip set into five 1¾"-wide segments.

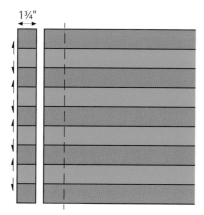

Cut 5 segments.

2. Using the same fabrics used in step 1, reverse the placement of the two colors when joining the 1¾" x 9" strips. Press the seam allowances toward the darker print. Cut the strips into four 1¾"-wide segments.

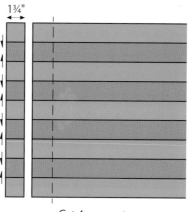

Cut 4 segments.

3. Sew the strip-set segments together, alternating them to make block A. Press the seam allowances in one direction. The block should measure 11¾" x 1 1¾". Repeat to make 14 A blocks total.

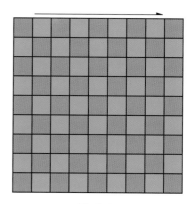

Block A.
Make 14.

Making the B Blocks

Referring to the photo on page 75, lay out 81 dark 1¾" squares randomly in nine horizontal rows of 9 squares each. Sew the squares in each row together. Press the seam allowances in opposite directions from row to row. Join the rows to make block B. Press the seam allowances in one direction. The block should measure 11¾" x 11¾". Repeat to make 42 B blocks total.

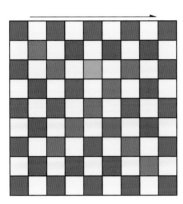

Block B.
Make 42.

Assembling the Quilt Top

1. Referring to the quilt assembly diagram on page 78, arrange the quilt top in eight horizontal rows of seven blocks per row. Follow the placement of A blocks and B blocks shown in the diagram below.

B	A	A	A	B	B	B
A	B	B	B	B	B	B
B	B	B	B	B	A	B
B	A	B	B	B	B	A
A	B	B	B	B	B	B
B	B	B	B	B	B	B
B	A	B	B	B	B	B
A	A	B	A	B	A	A

Block placement

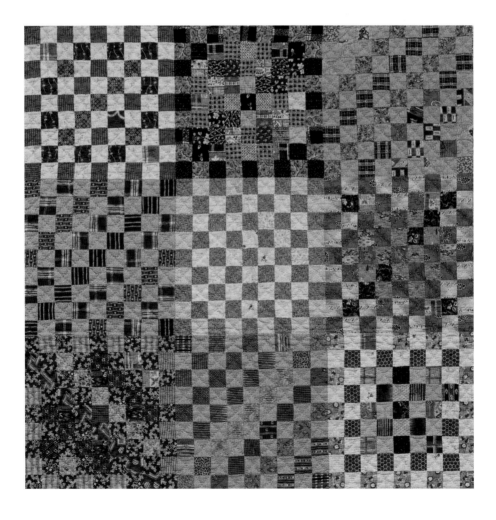

2. Sew the blocks together into rows, pressing the seam allowances in opposite directions from row to row.

3. Sew the rows together. Press the seam allowances in one direction.

Finishing the Quilt

For more information on finishing your quilt, go to ShopMartingale.com/HowtoQuilt.

1. Layer the backing, batting, and quilt top; baste.

2. Quilt as you wish. An X is hand quilted in brown thread through each square of this antique quilt.

3. Bind the quilt using the brown-stripe 2½"-wide strips.

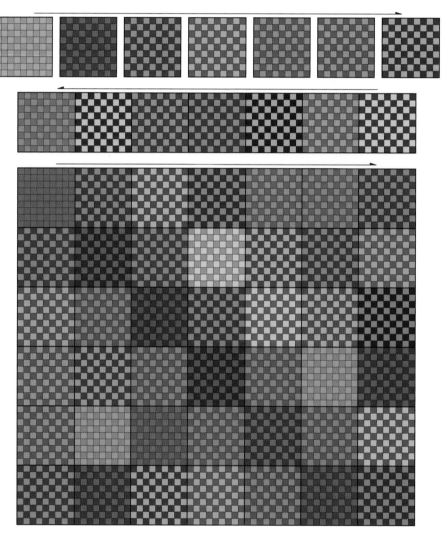

Quilt assembly

❧ Acknowledgments ❧

Owning a quilt shop and being in the quilting industry as a whole has given me many friends that have become like an extended family. It has been the best job.

A special thank-you to my friend Diane Rebholz for the many hours spent piecing and quilting.

Thanks to Jean Jacobson, neighbor and friend. We have made a lot of trips back and forth across the street planning, cutting, piecing, and quilting together. We also love to antique together—who doesn't love a flea market?

Thanks to Rod (Jean's husband) and Greg (my husband) for all the extra things they do for me. There are a lot of extra jobs that come with owning a quilt shop, and they probably wouldn't get done without these two.

Thanks to my son, Matt, and his wife, Amy. I refer to them as my IT and Marketing departments. I don't know what I would do without them. They are also mom and dad to my grandson, Alex. Being Alex's grandma is the best part of every day.

Thanks to Deb, Kaye, and Sue. We make a great team at JJ Stitches.

Finally, thanks to Mickey and Windham Fabrics for giving me the opportunity to use my antique quilt collection as an inspiration for designing reproduction fabrics.

❧ About the Author ❧

Julie Hendricksen has been collecting antique quilts for over 30 years. Scrap quilts from the turn of the 19th century are her favorites. As Julie professes, the more fabrics in each quilt, the more interesting they become!

Visitors to Julie's quilt shop, JJ Stitches in Sun Prairie, Wisconsin, will often find both a reproduction quilt and the antique quilt that inspired it on display together. Julie's collection of antique quilts is the inspiration for the fabric lines she's designed for Windham Fabrics, and it's no surprise that her shop specializes in reproduction fabrics.

Julie has presented many trunk shows around the Midwest to share both the antique quilts in her collection and the reproduction quilts made from them. Quilters are often surprised and excited to see 100 quilts laid out in front of them as they walk into the venue. Some of those attending didn't even know they loved scrap quilts or antique quilts until after the program. They are now some of her shop's best customers!

Remembering the Past is Julie's first book. Her quilts have been featured in *American Patchwork and Quilting, McCall's Quilting,* and *Primitive Quilts and Projects.*

Julie lives in De Forest, Wisconsin, with her husband, Greg. Son Matt and his wife, Amy, live nearby with grandson Alex.

Other Titles You Might Like

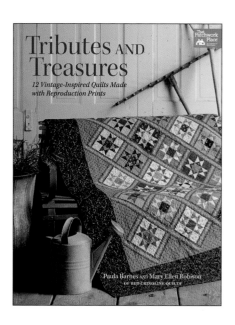

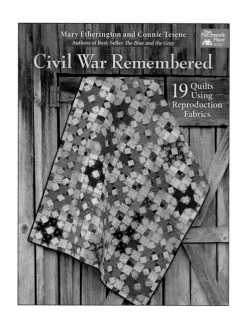

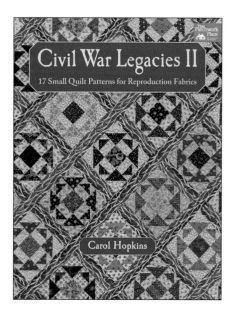

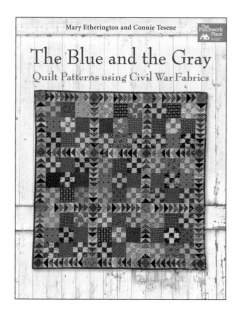